# OF LOVE, DEATH & THE SEA-SQUIRT

# CHRIS GREENHALGH

❊

# *Of* Love, *Death*
## *and the*
# Sea-Squirt

BLOODAXE BOOKS

ISBN: 1 85224 485 2

First published 2000 by
Bloodaxe Books Ltd,
P.O. Box 1SN,
Newcastle upon Tyne NE99 1SN.

Bloodaxe Books Ltd acknowledges
the financial assistance of Northern Arts.

*For Ruth, Saul and Ethan*

Cover printing by J. Thomson Colour Printers Ltd, Glasgow.

Printed in Great Britain by
Cromwell Press Ltd, Trowbridge, Wiltshire.

I vowed to abjure the word 'love', yet write of little else. Let us think of it as the spiritual twin of gravity – no crude force, 'exerted' by the planets in their orbits, but somehow simply, Einsteinly there, a mathematical property of space itself. Some people and places just make us feel heavier than others, is all.

JOHN UPDIKE, *A Month of Sundays*

# Acknowledgements

Acknowledgements are due to the editors of the following publications where some of these poems, or versions of them, first appeared: *The Gregory Anthology 1991-1993* (Sinclair-Stevenson, 1994), *New Blood* (Bloodaxe Books, 1999), *Poetry Durham* and *Southfields*. 'The Glass-Blower' was a 'highly commended' runner-up in the *Daily Telegraph* Arvon Poetry Competition. Along with 'The Last Seduction', it was published in the competition anthology, *The Ring of Words* (Sutton, 1998). 'Lisbon: Good Friday...' was a runner-up in the *TLS*/Blackwells Poetry Competition in 1998. 'Monkey Business' also achieved bridesmaid status in the same competition in 1999.

'A Man in the Valley of Women' owes much to Maxine Hong Kingston's story 'On Discovery' and Fellini's film *City of Women*. 'An Encounter' has its origin in Italo Calvino's 'A Soldier's Tale', and 'Monkey Business' borrows from Nabokov the observation of the monkey sketching the bars of its own cage.

Special thanks are due to my wife, Ruth, and to Chris Fletcher and Graham Majin, whose constant support and encouragement have helped make this book what it is.

# Contents

# A Short History of Milk

For days you collected milk bottles
until Saturday night
in broad pans, you gently heated the pints
and filled the bath voluptuously full.

Then you slipped, toe-first, into the warm
creamy liquid, and sank into your dreams –
imagining yourself as the warrior Queen,
Cleopatra, reclining with kittenish languor

in the Egyptian baths.
There you contemplated a swelling empire,
your body pure alabaster,
waiting in Oriental splendour for

your swarthy armour-plated lover,
Mark Antony, to join you in the waters,
wrap you in the skeins of his toga
and give you his fill of human kindness.

It was a while before I heard your screams.
At first I feared the worst: silky water
spilling over the sides of the bath,
rippling damply along the walls of the flat.

The truth was much stranger.
As it cooled, the milk underneath your
gently churning fingers had taken on a thick solidity,
become densely actual, and turned into butter.

Your skin enjoyed a dairy freshness.
Blue Roquefort veins shot through your breasts.
I slid you out and showered you down,
then towelled you dry from toe to crown.

I pressed you between the thin
white sheets of the bed, where you lay
sheathed like a soft cheese in muslin:
supple, mature, pungent; bright like the Milky Way.

9

## Footloose

I drink champagne from your slipper
then cook the shoe for supper –

a ragout made of the damask upper;
the sole minced, the heel cut into slices

and fried in butter...

Then I go to work on your toes:
burlesque, pawky, ogreish. God knows,

the skin is a little withered, the nails sharp,
but each little piggy goes to market

and each little piggy comes home.

# A Man in the Valley of Women

He was captured in the Valley of Women.
They manacled his ankles and chained his wrists.
His captors pinioned him. One held his head.
Another picked up a needle and thread.

'What are you going to do?' he asked.
She played the needle over a candle flame.
'Sew your lips together!' she laughed,
trailing a finger between his shoulder-blades.

She teased the needle through his upper lip,
and drew the flesh together with silk-twine.
He felt the pressure of her fingertips
as her nails dug deep into his spine.

Slowly they broke all the bones in his feet.
The blood was used to rouge his cheeks.
His testes made an executive toy,
his glans a novelty cork for the wine.

Seized by the throes of change, he was aware
of a contending self, radically other;
an abrupt warping, a cruel deflection
of his sex from masculine to feminine.

The next few months, they fed him on jasmine
which stirred the female wings inside his breasts.
His ankles grew slimmer. His hair shone.
His vagina fermented like yeast.

A musk clung to his body. Unmistakable.
His clitoris thickened like a tonsil.
Buttermilk and aloe dissolved his Adam's apple.
His voice modulated to a falsetto.

They plucked every dark hair from his face
and pencilled his eyebrows until they were perfect.
They painted his lips in arresting shades,
and squeezed him into a whalebone corset.

11

Finally, he was ready for the Queen's birthday.
His hips swivelled pertly, his backside swayed.
'*Tsk tsk!*' went the other courtiers slyly.
'That's a frisky one,' he heard them say.

He burst from the cake, high-kicking through the icing,
swanking bridally from the marzipan.
Later, the Queen bid him kiss her ring.
She sighed: 'To think that once you were a man...'

# Augustus John

You old goat, Augustus John!
The way you patted children on
the head, just in case they were your own!

You had only to see the sun
touch the protein in a girl's hair,
had merely to glimpse the shallow concavity
of a woman's abdomen,

or be drawn into her fragrant zone,
to feel a quickening tingle, a sweet ache of distension,
a remote throb of semi-engorgement,
a shocked little pang tighten inside your pants.

Remember the Swiss girl who came to your door?
Afterwards, surveying the broken banister,
the pool of blood, the pile of sugar,
you exclaimed, 'There's been a bit of a kerfuffle!'

Later, in the hospital, when she had recovered,
you boasted
one night of love with you was enough
to bring any woman back from the dead.

Increasingly arthritic, you couldn't
hold steady a brush or a pen,
but lordly over each kneeling fellatrice,
the one thing you could command –

boneless, amatory, free-standing –
would rise the way a motionless body, mortally cold,
would rise at the bidding of a great healer.
And, Lazarene, you rose as often as the sun.
You old goat, Augustus John!

# The Vengeful Wife

Soporific, epically gorged, I sit back,
licking my fingers clean of their grease,

leaving a tidemark of eroded lipstick
scarved around each one.

I gather my souvenirs:
a few porcine hairs,

two gold teeth, a gall-stone,
a wedding ring, one char-grilled heart,

his eyes, which I place in a pickle-jar
high on a shelf (the cap screwed on tight),

a meshed saddle of fat...
In slivers, I feed his tongue to the cat.

# Gift of the Gag

And even if I did
cut off your tongue –

the other indefatigable muscle
in your body –

it would flicker silverly,
slither like a lizard

and strain soundlessly
towards some glib defence

of the indefensible.
In the silence,

your words hang inadequately,
traces over the quick of the world.

## Of Love, Death and the Sea-Squirt

Hoping publicly to humiliate her husband,
she filmed herself swallowing whiskey and pills.

That night, watching in snowy low-grade colour
his wife's self-slaughter reproduced,

he fast-forwarded through all the abuse,
but stopped when she spoke of the sea-squirt,

listening with a sympathetic taste of acid on his tongue
to details of the creature's life-long

search for a rock to make its home;
then the hideous consummation

as it set about eating its own brain.
That was the only part he watched again.

# Monkey Business

Two glass bubble-lifts rose noiselessly behind you,
up through the atrium of the hotel.
I introduced myself, reading your name-tag slyly –
at a perky angle to your chest.

Delivering my paper, I avoided your gaze.
My first slide showed me coaxing the monkey
into holding a pencil, trying to make it draw.
The next disclosed how, once I withdrew,

the animal took up the pencil and drew the world it saw:
the iron bars of its cage!
That night, I retired to my room – separate,
but connecting with yours.

Resisting the impulse to remove the key from the door
and monitor your behaviour,
I was soon asleep, imagining richly your
hair coming down, your dress slipping off,

an arm of your glasses teased between your teeth
as you slid into bed with a piece of research.
A fragment of Paradise blundered upon.
Just you and me like Adam and Eve.

The next day, there you were standing at the lectern,
one stockinged foot loosed from a shoe, caressing
the calf of your other leg, the OHP transparency
casting gloopy shadows, formulae

scrolling across the screen and your body
like your own genetic code.
Chatting afterwards over drinks, a green olive
hung in my Martini like a red-irised reptile eye.

As you drank, I saw the butterfly-shaped blackness
at the back of your throat.
I was thinking *angel*. You were thinking *missing link*;
the worm in the tequila bottle monstrously evolved;

the hummingbird, wings vibrating, poised above
a flower with its tongue.
I left you talking to an oceanographer. All night long,
I suffered the sounds of love from your room.

The bark of seals. The slap of waves. Whale song.

# In the Aquarium

Washed by glaucous shadows,
electrified by the *tsig tsig tsig*

of stockinged legs,
I kiss you, and a fish

glides across your iris
like the sliver of colour in a marble –

your tongue swimming lightly
inside my mouth, where

a taut bubble of ecstasy
in slow-motion explodes.

# At the Gezirah Club

Hardly had I stepped off the plane onto a metal staircase
and inhaled the hot brume of a humid night –
scarcely had I entered the nightclub where
fluorescent light fell like tickertape across the bar,

than I was sitting with you at the pool in the Gezirah Club,
stirring an iced drink with my finger,
dangling my legs in the water
and watching shadows mutate on the tiles.

A tender wishbone of skin
glistened above your swim-suit.
The slim wet prints of your high-arched feet
revealed just how little of our bodies

actually touch the ground;
our ankles, pivots for some effort of flight.
Sprinklers ticked on the golf-course.
A diving-board vibrated in the light.

Your mother was playing the ninth and final hole
(the course cut by Nasser to accommodate a race-track
in 1954). Enjoying considerable luck,
she had gone round the first eight in under 30.

The sun shone with the intensity of a welding torch
as you confided that, if you died,
you could be identified by the pale patch
beneath your Nefertiti pendant

and the white of your backside.
I asked if it was true here that physicians
spent much of their time sewing up the hymens
of eligible girls, healing them into virgins again.

Torn rainbows of spray fanned from the sprinklers.
Blushing, you spilled your drink on the water,
its stain spreading to cover our reflections,
softening our contours into a blur.

Words rose to your throat in strings of vertical bubbles,
only to remain like the taut globes of air
rising through the pool, unbroken...
At that moment, your mother came over,

the unexpected tension of a smile on her face,
the shaft of her golf-club glinting in the sun,
one arm raised in triumph; the ball
held like a trophy between finger and thumb.

# Love

Some things you just know.
Sitting in the revolving restaurant,
Seeing the city like a photograph, slowly exposed,

I depress the plunger on the cafetière:
A detonation in slow-motion,
Grains enlivened and shoaled.

The room's angles tilt, its space redrawn.
The rim-pattern on my plate begins to spin.
A variable gravity enters the fabric of things.

Somehow, objects are sustained,
Silently upheld, pushed upwards
By a pressure unseen –

Like the bridge in the distance,
Each end dissolved in mist,
Its suspension miraculous.

# The Vision Thing

Sitting in the optician's chair
while she leans close and shines
a pencil-torch onto my cornea,

I am included in the intimacy
of the aroma the cloud of her hair gives off.
Her gravity impinges on me

with the weight of trespass.
Close-up, the plane of her cheek resembles
the photograph of a planet's surface.

'Is it better like this... or this?'
Atoms jiggle as I squinny
through dreamlike thicknesses of glass.

The knit of the visible world stretches thin.
Revealed details warp as though broken...
Outside, lines which previously never met

now begin to intersect.
Snowflakes bloom chrysanthemumesque
in car headlights, their strangeness renewed.

And when in a department store later
I see you on the escalator
rise frictionlessly against the mirrors –

surrounded by the contending odours
of the perfume counter –
I almost swoon.

# Tact

Later, I was surprised to find,
on the margin of some papers,

the image of your photocopied hand –
its grainy ghost of fingers

flattened in a plane of shadow,
the palm scored with lines.

I pressed my own hand
to embrace yours and,

as if a chemical had dropped,
felt somewhere our fingers chastely conjoin;

the contact like a kiss given so high up
we each receive an electric shock.

As from obscurely rippled water, an image stirred,
the molecules oddly stacked:

that first night when we stood, naked, kissing,
our hands, as agreed, behind our backs.

# My Funny Valentine

Those first days, making love above your father's study,
he would cough
so often in synchrony with your bliss
as to suggest a certain psychic discomfort.

I still remember that Valentine's, he took us out to dinner:
some high-priced, low-ceilinged Italian place.
As a waiter waggled a huge pepper-mill over
our plates, abruptly the pressure of the unspoken

broke. The word 'marriage' was broached
with the deft solemnity of a man handling high-grade uranium.
After several glasses of wine, we all began to glow.
A blue vein pulsed at his temple as he spoke.

Hypnotised by the wax dripping from the candle
and congealing between my fingers,
I conjured *a garlicky moon, a suitcase,*
*you squeezing through the windowframe,*

*the lemonstain headlamps of the Citroën*
*strafing the walls of your parents' bedroom*
*before tilting into the night*...Outside,
snow pecked at the window. The shadows

of leaves made flat dark hearts against the wall.
The web of wax between my fingers cracked.
The candle flames staggered in a sudden draught,
your eyes picking up flecks of yellow as gold.

My legs twitched like a pinioned insect's.
And sure enough, by the spring,
the light struck rainbows off your diamond ring.
By the summer we were married and, by the fall,

your operatic cries of joy
might have been heard by the neighbours
but for the double-glazed caulked storm-windows
prudently installed against the winter cold.

25

## Without a Thought

Without a thought for a tip
or the taxi door,
we raced up the path to my house,
hand-in-hand.
Without a thought for the letters
fanned on the floor
or messages on the answering-machine
we leapt up the stairs,
hand-in-hand.
Without a thought for the cat
or the flowers dying of thirst,
we moved towards the bedroom
where our breath bloomed in the dark...
Because we were warm,
hand-in-hand,
with each other.
And we began to undress –
without a thought for the curtains
or the neighbours,
without a thought for the creases
in our discarded clothes.
Naked, we led each other to bed,
our bodies twisting in moonlight,
my hands in your hands,
pressed above your head.

# Miscarriage

I should have known.
That morning, the milk-float spilled its load
across the road.
The moon tremored like an embryo.

On the train, stations sped by
like improbable Christian names.
The rails slid together behind us
towards their vanishing point.

Inside the hospital, it was too hot.
The scan showed a grainy radar blip.
Nothing inside.
Just a clot of blood.

Doctors listened for an echo no longer there.
Your face crumpled darkly like a flower.
Tears formed second lenses over your eyes.
The red lights of a transmitter shivered distantly.

Back home, I consigned
the uncollected train tickets to the bin.
Jets of water pressed against the shower-curtain
with the pressure of tiny fingers...

Next morning – the wonder of it – how things
go on being themselves.
An unwashed milk bottle holds its ghost inside.
First buds appear on the narcissi.

# The Glass-Blower

A month after the miscarriage,
we watch a glass-blower
fill himself full of puff
and breathe life into dead space.

A bubble pullulates from a knot –
a hot celestial drop –
into a gaseous envelope,
a molten clotted globe,
enjoying its buoyancy,
sustaining its miracle of self-belief
until its wobbling elongating film
grows taut as a raindrop
in its transparent caul.

The room grows smaller and smaller
as the limpid bubble's membranous sac
stretches clear to the ceiling,
staggering elastically as it lengthens and cools.

I imagine for a moment
all the vitreous flasks
breaking through the wall,
floating free and letting fall
a host of glaucous bubbles –
hovering over the city like
swarms of soapy cherubim,
clinging airily to
the surface of the river
then popping one after another –
like the souls which
make themselves known
at night as drops of water,
distilling at the warm touch of a face.

And if one definition of an angel
is that it takes up no space,
then you were blessed:
a luminous trace in the memory.

The touch of fingers in
the dark and silence –
undiscovered,
unknowable, unnamed.

# Exposure

I come home to find you peeling onions,
removing layer upon layer of papery skin –

the thin transparent films
Balzac feared he would shed

each time his photograph was taken.
Slivers of violet and gold blacken

in scalding oil.
Your eyes wobble.

Tears shake into the pan and hiss.
A tremulous vapour drifts

out the window and into the air
like the final unrecoverable essence

of the self, leaving the image of a skeleton:
the tender negative of a finger,

the wedding ring floating eerily
like a halo around the white bone.

# Two in the Twilight
*(after Montale)*

Between you and me on the gazebo
unfolds a membranous darkness
that slow-wipes the hills' outline
and, more importantly, your face.

You stand, bereft of your gestures.
The air opens only to devour
each of our steps here
in the dark.

I no longer recognise anything of myself.
Even the movement of my head
and the sound of my own voice
seem alien and strange.

The wind stirs. The dark trees shake.
The first lights pick out the pier.
Words fall awkwardly between us.
I look at you with renewed fear.

I do not feel as though I know you.
This I know: that never
was I further from you
than in this late hour.

A few moments have cauterised everything.
Everything except two faces –
two death-masks that allow themselves
the brief carving of a smile.

# The Story of the Senhora de O

I don't believe in miracles, but
that day in Lamego
you made me take your photo
in front of the Senhora de O:

a blatantly pregnant version of the Virgin Mary.
You nursed your stomach the way,
burnished by worshipful kisses,
the statue did in its alcove.

Then in the afternoon came three signs.
By the pool you found a four-leaf clover.
A bird shat on your camera.
And the self-testing kit you purchased earlier

showed two blue lines instead of one.
The following day in the museum
we looked at the tapestries: I dwelt upon
Laius consulting the oracle

being told he'd first be killed
then cuckolded by his son.
You preferred the threadbare religious triptych
featuring the Annunciation, the Visitation

and the Presentation in the Temple.
I don't believe in miracles
but since that day in Portugal
you've prayed for a baby boy, I a baby girl.

# Gift

A fierce wave knocks off my glasses,
leaving me dazed and breathless,
the glistening crescents of the lenses
wrestling brilliances in the undertow
where a used condom spores
like an engorged Portuguese man o'war.
The receding water
leaves a hot little pool
in which salt and light and protein mix.
Along with my glasses, I see these gifts:
two dolls' heads, a bottle,
a few opalescent scallop shells
and the saturated hull
of a man's left plimsoll –
doubtless brought here from Newfoundland
by the North Atlantic Drift
to settle on this remote stretch of sand
in Cornwall. Astonishingly, it fits.
And like the oar which seems broken in water
then instantly heals as you lift it clear,
I see the light – a fantasised sibling
losing his footing
and sending this sign
across the ocean
to loll like the vitreous body
of a dead fish, rising
then falling, rising and falling
according to the whims of the tide.

## After a Certain Silence

We enjoy being touched from above,
by rain, snow,
a benevolent hand, as though
the quotation marks had fallen from the word 'love'.

'Love', for which there exists a poverty
of rhymes in the English language,
though we do have a giant chalk image of a man with an erection
carved into the hills.

And typical, you remark, of men –
the controllers of language –
to abrogate the first human note for themselves:
*Dada dada dada...*

In a dressing-gown, wet-haired after a bath,
you apply a few scribbles of moisturising lotion
as if putting on a new layer of skin.
Upstairs, sleeps our eleven-month-old son.

Reluctant to stop nursing him,
you are still so brimful of milk that,
jarred, you might spill.
We listen to the intercom,

alert to his every stirring movement,
tense for each amplified snag
in his breathing,
as though to a broadcast from another world.

# That Summer

Twistingly, the road rose above us,
broken into foreshortened slices,
flickering half-eclipsed amid the hills.

Next to me, your finger
traced the road on the map
as if following a whorl of grain on furniture.

Mist lifted like the tissue page in a Bible.
A huge sky slid into place.
Abruptly, an oncoming car

slewed across our side of the road.
My foot slammed down hard on the brake
which responded morbidly in the wet.

I felt the cradle of my seatbelt stretch
as its length unspooled,
then tighten and take hold.

Hedgerows leaped forward as the car,
twisted by the torque
of the warped road, spun around.

A stillness distended until
we became conscious, almost,
of the turning of the earth –

your face, a moon
tinted green in the windscreen,
as if by a sense of merge giving on

the face of our young son in the back:
timorous, wary, alert to the swerve
as though tugged into another universe.

# Mothering Sunday

'It's where the money is,' declared my neighbour –
a man who would circulate at parties
and pass round notes bearing the legend:
*Love Unselfishly...*

My wife sat in the kitchen nursing our baby,
adjusting the strap on her bare shoulder,
the sting of one breast bared like Colette.
'She's very photogenic,' he went on,

setting the perforations over the sprockets
before clicking the back of his camera shut.
'And they'd be tastefully done...'
He slid his finger along my bookshelves:

Lawrence, Miller, Nabokov, Anaïs Nin,
then shaped his hands like a pyramid below his chin.
Above his fingers, his eye shone
like the emblem on a dollar bill.

Steadfastly, I gazed at the television.
Somewhere in the States, a crowd had gathered,
devotional eyes upturned to where
the spindrift from the sprinklers had projected

a hologram of the Madonna onto an office block.
My wife, in the next room, closed her ruckled blouse
and opened the fridge door with its drawings in crayon:
a man, a woman, a house and two cars.

'No one will find out. I promise, Graham.'
Bubbles of stale water formed around the stems
of flowers in their vase.
Moments later, he was gone, leaving the door still open.

# Aquacity

I swim alone –
a dense effortful churning in the blue of the hotel pool.
Of the two broad poolside windows,
one gives onto the eager resinous tang of spring,

the other onto the gym
where, also alone, a young woman plies an exercise bike.
A bubble surrounds everything.
Idly, her arms hang at either side,

her fingers trailing experimentally as though
from the low sides of a boat.
Sweat trickles down her throat.
The thinnest of gold necklaces glimmers

beneath a few errant strands of long blonde hair.
Soon, her shirt adheres tackily to her back
revealing, through the airy weave of fibres,
the white shadow of a bra.

She rides, tightly wound like a musical box which will,
any minute, spring into bliss.
The cords at her neck elongate until
the taut strings of the bike sustain a high thrilling note.

Finishing, she sips from a dinky Styrofoam cup
(water so cold it makes your teeth throb),
leaving a vivid lipstick stain on the rim.
The lines of the swimming pool jiggle beneath me.

An ectoplasm of shadows laps fantastically on the ceiling,
contributing to the sense of chemical event.
Afterwards, in the foyer,
clouds of hair fluffed wide from a shower,

she walks: humid, perfumed, unpossessable...
Tomorrow, I will be on a plane.
I know that were I to see her again,
it would be in another time, another place.

And as the jet in my imagination steeply banks
above the roseate spokes of the city –
each bridge a double strand of diamonds,
each suburb a scarf of pearls –

the memory of my time here enjoys a heightened gloss:
the mirrory glitter of the buildings;
sunset colouring the snow-topped mountains
like the tender smudge of lipstick on that cup.

The city shrinks in diminishing perspective
beneath the broad white wing,
touched with splendour, like the crossed legs of the air hostesses
now strapping themselves in for take-off.

# Turbulence

Your grip on my hand tightened
as the engines took hold –
a sustained tumultuous roar
that seemed to come from within me
and be given to the air...

Through the scratched windows, we saw
ourselves lifted hugely.
The ground spread itself like a map
beneath us.

Cars moved with an odd perfection
as though on rails.
A swimming pool glimmered
like one superb blue tear.
The city dwindled to a toy-town
as, gently tugged, slowly blown,
we put an angelic distance
between ourselves and the world.

My ears clicked.
A blood-vessel in your nose tripped.
In front of us, a young boy
took two deep puffs from an inhaler
and felt the benevolent swerve of atoms
agitate kindly inside his mouth.

Later, unbuckled, nursing a whiskey,
the smudged whorls of my thumb
loomed ogreishly through the sides of a glass.
The drink tilted, the liquid shifted in my ears.
Bits of skyey water flashed below.

Pouring westwards against the sunset,
the rose glow of the earth stained
the white underside of the jet.
It was then you led me
by a single finger to the toilet,
and, like a humid cloud descending,

sat astride me
in the classic position
of Penelope consoling Ulysses.

Lights winked on the wing-tips.
Below us brimmed cities.
Above us, stars.

# Morning in the Hotel

The clean scent of your hair
spills off the pillow –

damp, vitaminised, your green eyes
the milky colour of cut flower stems.

You slide out of bed and pad
towards the shower where your skin

pinkens under the pour of water
like a hand held close beneath the beam of a torch.

Through the cubicle's smoky glass,
I see you wreathed in steam;

a rocket on the launch pad
about to rise clear into the stratosphere,

leaving me still in bed,
like the awed and sunstruck crowd,

who, stretching out their fingers
as though to touch the stars,

find their inner spaces drained,
their bodies cruelly unlifted.

# Lisbon: Good Friday, Looking Westwards

Under the yellow segments of a parasol
canted to catch the sun's last rays, we sit
drinking water – hysterically fizzy, turbid with bubbles,
slices of lemon enjoying the zest of stars.

The blonde polleny down on your legs
is a sore reminder of my hay fever.
Thirty-four and never before a sufferer,
suddenly I'm allergic to the histrionic growth of spring.

You ask me if I'm tired of being a husband, father...
Stung into stubborn silence, I scan the horizon.
Even with my hopeless sense of direction,
I know that beyond lie the Azores, then the Americas.

Close by, a policeman on a podium
presides over the traffic the way
the Rio-like statue of Christ, palms open,
blesses the length of the suspension bridge.

Jesus, supreme musician of the world, summons
and holds the long motorised note,
the vehicular hum across the Tagus.
Above us, planes come in low over the houses,

the skeletons of angels; while before us,
wonderfully mongrelised, reconciling
the shapes of a sword, a cross and a prow
stands the Monument to the Discoveries:

Henry the Navigator. Magellan.
Vasco da Gama. Luis de Camões –
who, the ship going down and forced to choose
between his wife who couldn't swim

and his imperishable manuscript,
heaved with one free hand towards the shore
while holding, in the other,
his book aloft above the water...

Our life together has been full of small tremors.
Like the good people of Lisbon,
we live on a line of seismic convulsion,
hoping the big one will never happen.

This time, it's me who says I'm sorry first.
Nearby, a fountain explodes
like a flock of birds into swift motion.
The ceaseless gentle impact of water upon stone.

# The Fan

The fan clicks round into this corner of the room,
its blue fluted blades stirring my hair,

levelling my thoughts to the same plane
of remoteness as the wheels of a motorcycle

on a ride undertaken long ago.
My lashes shimmer to reveal a picnic:

blood-oranges, a wine bottle, quarters of melon.
An unassimilated bit of tanning lotion

glistens on your belly like an iota of solar spit,
melting like a poll of dandelion

into the bleached space of salty lips
and burning kisses – a spotted blaze of sunlight

complexly fitted to the spokes dissolving back
through the blur of years

to the urgent pressure of the present:
the rotary motion of the fan

as it plays upon my iris; the wind on our faces
dwindling to the cool blue strobe of blades

agitating the shadows of leaves on my desk.
My cheeks catch something of

the faded heat of the event.
My eyes swarm with sunlight and I sneeze.

# Under the Volcano

Maddened by the lamps,
mosquitoes swarm
in a halo of fluorescence.

Their electrocutions set the nerves
on edge.
Dead husks litter the ground

and crackle like sugar underfoot.
A brilliantined waiter empties
trayful after trayful into the bin...

And as though they had delved
with their sooty fingers
into the second circle of Hell,

archaeologists pull up the charred, heraldic,
perfectly preserved features
of a couple arrested in the act –

like lovers in a suicide pact
having swallowed match
after match after match...

Delicately they brush off the wings
of dust and ash to reveal
the blackened couple

in the shocked tenderness
of a last passionate embrace.
Soldered at the hip, and with lips

plugged together, their petrified effigy
is recovered from the bath-house
in full view of the Bay –

their emblazoned faithfulness
declaring what death
could not remove

and what the scorched couple
in their everlasting clasp will always have:
the pathos of tenacious love.

# Reading Between the Lines

It is right that the philosophy section of the library
should be located on the top floor
where two biographers, unbeknown to each other,
work on the same definitive life.

There's talk of a cache of love poems
addressed to a secret mistress
extending over thirty years
and talk, too, of Nazi sympathies.

The two write with Freudian omnivorousness
of birth, war, death and sex,
while a few miles away, the subject's wife and executrix
feeds his letters to the shredder.

Later, both will comment on the irony of this.
One will liken the strips of paper
to the fronds of a plant freed to the air; the other
to the fingers of a man slipping from a precipice.

# Coco and Igor

*Born a little over a year from each other and dying in the same year, 1971, Coco Chanel and Igor Stravinsky lived long and intriguingly parallel lives, enjoying a brief affair in 1920 – the year Chanel No.5 was invented. The sympathy which their relationship seems to embody is sounded here.*

Igor sits, cutting his toe-nails –
a scatter of hard crisp little moons
the colour of old piano keys,

his bald pate mottled in the rich detailing
thrown by the lamp above the mirror.
His glasses steal glitter

from the lights, catching the vibration
of red wine on the table,
showing to advantage its smoky tones.

\*

Colognes, unguents, fragrant pomades,
atomisers, faceted jars and dye-pots:
the collected sweat of the gods!

Coco opens a flacon of perfume
lifting the cut-glass stopper with a twist,
releasing a mist of scent across her wrist.

Tilting her head back amorously
she dabs with a single finger
a smidgen along her throat,

relishing the crinkly sound
and sparky crackle of her petticoat
as it rubs against the silk of her gown.

\*

A piece of tailor's chalk.
A muffled crunch of scissors.
A scalloped neckline, an ellipse of pearls.

He pervades her like a melody.
She penetrates him like a scent.
The interpenetration of his Russian, her French accent.

*

Thin tapering strips of light shoot in
through half-open shutters,
breaking in bars across Coco's body,

improvising a shadowy keyboard
the length of her naked back,
where Igor's tendony fingers trail

in a series of wondrous contacts.
A delicious salinity flows from her skin,
bewitching him. Drunk on her musk,

he answers to something tender within her.
A glow diffuses itself longsufferingly
like an odour across her throat –

as though the felt hammers of a piano
had sustained a jubilant note.
His body throbs like a violin

rubbed completely with the whole length of the bow,
followed by a moment of slow dissolution,
a hopelessly poignant making-of-itself-small.

The dust falls in luminous silence.
The light lends everything edges,
making them warm.

# Scandal
*(for Graham Majin)*


A careless remark over dinner
repeated idly in the newsroom
makes three column inches in the local *Chronicle,*
finds itself a feature article
in the evening editions
where it is picked up by syndicated news organisations

and sent down the wires
to be broadcast repeatedly
on first local then national radio and TV
before attracting the attentions
of the foreign press with banner headlines in
*Le Figaro, La Repubblica, Die Welt, El Pais,*

and presently its imperishable echo
spins westwards over the Atlantic
where it leaks through cracks in the ocean floor,
penetrates the earth's core
and fetches up in Reykjavik –
the whispering of millions swelling epically to

a storm, carrying it like a virulent spirochete
all the way to the Americas,
through New York, Boston, Connecticut,
hurrying on beyond the Great Lakes to the Mid West
where the story takes on a new twist
and from there across the desert to California

where it catches on a satellite dish
like a hysterically sustained coloratura
and is bounced to distant galaxies
in heaven-opening hallelujahs
finally coming to rest on a fugitive alien antenna
one million light years away.

# An Encounter

The woman seated next to me in the carriage
gazed unblinkingly out the window,
her hands folded tightly on the purse in her lap.

A snowflake, stuck to the glass, snagged
with a miracle of trembling
in the reflection of her lashes.

In a series of minute adjustments,
I fitted myself next to her; a light contact
broken then re-established by each new sway of the train.

Slyly, my leg came to rest against hers
while my fingers with deft infinitesimal gestures,
through my trousers, reconnoitred her thigh.

All the while, she stared ahead absently,
her hands still clasped on the purse in her lap,
her fingers poised on its metal catch.

As we entered the tunnel, I took my chance.
One hand advanced along her leg.
The other groped through thicknesses of cloth.

My mouth sought the hotness of her throat.
Her head fell languidly upon my shoulder.
Her hands slipped from her lap.

A train flashed by in one continuous stripe.
Re-emerging into the light,
her eyes still stared ahead.

I felt the cold of her cheek, the limpness of her leg,
the absence of her breath against my neck.
Abruptly, I realised: she was dead.

# Exemplum

The thing is: it is necessary
sometimes to die
in order for people to suspect
your existence...

One morning, she arranged
the magnetic set of letters
on the refrigerator
into a suicide note.

After a month had gone by
and nobody had seen her,
two slovenly members of the local police
drove over and forced an entry.

They saw these things grouped together:
an electric fan and a glass of water,
multi-coloured strips of flypaper,
a refrigerator with a bass hum

and an eccentric ex-pat
lying dead on the kitchen floor of her villa
littered with the droppings of her
three hundred pets.

# Cultural Contact

English, French, Spanish – graduates mostly,
down-at-heel all, pursuing the cruel necessity
of employment in a slump – we travelled in convoy
from the toe to the crown of Italy.

Sales teams were formed according to
star-sign compatibility.
Dropped off on territory,
we operated like a virus on whole rows of shops.

For the first time, I understood capitalism:
the necessity to implicate oneself in the sale,
the need to generate a sense of fun,
the fetishism of music, travel, fashion...

One did well not to deviate from the sales patter:
a series of triggers demanding the word 'Yes',
so that, when it came to clinching the order,
'No' stuck like a fish-bone in the client's throat.

The 'works' (never 'encyclopaedias' – a prohibited word)
might, or might not, eventually arrive:
out-of-date, remaindered; the photographs
egregiously blurry or upside down –

like the screenings in the outdoor cinemas at night...
Bottles rolling down the aisles, cats screaming in heat.
Later, down at the discotheque on the beach,
we would go wild, drinking in relief

at the end of the week; dancing under an
unseasonable blizzard of lights –
a Babylonish mixingness, vehement, obscene.
And further off, like the slow sound of a cymbal, the sea.

The sea, and the recklessness that it attracts:
the apparition of buttocks swelling over the sand,
like the moon scampering backwards
through blanched and ragged clouds.

# An Englishman's Home

*(for Chris Fletcher)*


Prompted by a spate of burglaries,
you changed all the locks.
Now, entry depends on a coded knock.

Harlequin shards of glass line the wall.
The property enjoys Ivy League Security:
Chubb, Yale...

Hooked to a bank of monitors,
a series of cameras rake the perimeter fence.
Inside, an invisible grid

of laser-lines threatens, when penetrated,
to trip a clamorous alarm and bring
squad-cars yammering down the avenues,

a police helicopter pivoting in slow circles
around a single spot,
and a shit-hot SWAT team abseiling

down the sides of your home.
Still, robbers operate like shadows
on the underside of your mind.

Each night, you lie awake, tortured by the thought
that in the morning you will rise to find
everything you own, gone.

And when they do eventually come –
as come they must –
goaded by the aura of impregnability,

they will take nothing valuable:
no silver or jewels,
but, rather, all the light bulbs, the kettle,

the postcards from the mantel,
your *SAS Guide to Urban Survival*,
twelve toilet rolls and a bottle of Bell's, half-full.

# In the City

Rocking back in my predecessor's chair
where the brown smudge of his suicide
is still inauspiciously visible,
I put my feet up on the table.

To the left, a helipad on a hotel roof,
two costive businessmen holding down their ties.
To the right, for window-cleaning cage,
read industrial espionage.

Below, a man addresses a cash-machine like a lectern.
Two workmen carrying a huge mirror
catch a bright fragment of sky.
A sign! Like half a reflected cloud

perfectly matching the other half of a cloud
beyond the building's edge.
Like the rhythm of lit office windows
broken into bits of code.

Or the racks of shoes in high street shops,
the one, sinister, shoe on display.
Around me, pot-plants, vaguely tropical, obscurely lush
articulate a statement about the law of the jungle...

Returning late to the office,
I have reason to be suspicious
when I see the computer's screen-saving blue fish
churn lugubriously on my boss's desk.

I hear the photocopier in the back,
and recognise its blinding flash.
I even feel the patch of heat on the misted glass
where the secretary had sat. And all that

comes to mind is money: a Roman prodigality of coin;
notes watermarked with a faintly marbled pattern,
their tight whorls wrinkly as the river's sunk reflections
of advertisements and stars.

# Signs of the Times

### I

*The clouds methought would open, and show riches*
*Ready to drop upon me, that when I waked*
*I cried to dream again.*
THE TEMPEST

In the preferred version of the story
a rescue team, searching in
the honey-coloured light of dawn
amid unbuckled suitcases, fragments
of riveted fuselage, clinkered aluminium
and a darkly gesticulating alphabet
of arms, legs, breasts and heads,
come across the mottled bony fingers
of a severed hand arrested
in a fierce grip around a piece of paper.

Unfurling the stiffened fist, they discover –
who would credit it? –
the six multi-million-pound-winning numbers
of a National Lottery Ticket.

### II

Consider this: a Saturday
and a crowd gathers
outside an electrical store
to watch a man take a penalty.

Simultaneously, on twenty-five sets,
the striker strokes the ball
upon the referee's whistle
into the top left-hand corner of the net,

except on the twenty-sixth, a glitch –
some indeterminate swerve of matter
allowing the goalkeeper
miraculously to tip the ball over the bar!

## Shadowplay

Alexandria was badly hit during the war,
but a conjurer
recruited by the camouflage section
did the trick, concealing the real city
with khaki-coloured paint
and abracadabrising a fake with lights and mirrors.

The German bombers took the bait
and the whole mock-up wobbled like a mirage
with each new raid.
Each night the hoax city was rigged with craters
to authenticate the damage.
It was the same officer who out-foxed Rommel

with the jiggery-pokery of a thousand cardboard tanks.
He returned to the stage after the war,
somewhat disillusioned.
The night he collapsed during his act
of a heart attack,
the audience was in convulsions at his latest stunt.

Magicked away behind the curtains,
his heart bloomed
like an endless string of coloured handkerchiefs
until there were none left to draw upon.
Finger by finger, they removed his white gloves.
His soul rose noiselessly like a dove.

## Staying Alive

The sun falls nobly on its own sword.
Leaves fall singly, unobserved.
The caged bird,

as its migratory season nears,
dashes its head against the bars.
Spiders cry in the dark.

Stepping into the shower,
I ritually bend to taste my knee,
and remind myself

that the secret of immortality
is to treat each day
as a day impossible to die upon.

I feel the thin vortical draw of water
beneath my feet.
One great hemispherical leap

to our great white Queen
watching the War Lords
in their ostentatious penis-gourds

dance for rain.

# The Resurrection Project

Heat-wobble. Telescoped in a man's dark glasses,
a jet soars overhead.
The tail-fins of planes shark around the terminal.
Two thickset men whisper into their wrists.

On an impulse, the man strides, dark-suited
and with a valise, towards the figure of a chauffeur
who stands with a sign saying BROWN.
Seconds later, the real Brown emerges bewildered.

Synchronously, in separate locations
five assassinations are carried out:
on a golf course, in a laboratory,
a church library, a planetarium and a cable-car.

Inch by inch, detectives piece together
an unholy alliance of Italian mafiosi
and televangelists in the USA
who have acquired DNA from the Turin shroud.

A wizened nun speaks of the third secret of Fatima.
A Monsignor opens a locked drawer in the Vatican.
The plot-lines dovetail to one final messianic moment
when Christ is cloned and quickened

from just a few fugitive molecules on a stage…
But for now, let's stick with 'Brown'
gingerly opening his valise in the back of the stretch limo,
test tubes jiggling, reflected in his shades.

# News from the Sky

It is the day before Easter.
A man comes to the door offering to sell me
An aerial photograph of my own house.

Returning home tonight,
I feel for the key, its bitten silhouette cool,
Its little weight adamant in my hand.

Turning on the switches,
Filling the windows with light,
I think of the photograph,

Remote like a mosaic tile
Seen through water,
The road slowly identifiable as my own.

And I traces the sinews of contingency
Which have delivered me here,
Imagining myself as seen from above

In this house; one among thousands
In the town; the town a dot on
The country's map; the country

A smudge on the moist blue earth
And the earth a smithereen of dust and gas
In the inflationary wastes of space.

A light bulb pings in the silence.
The pattern on the wallpaper swarms.
Stars melt like snowflakes in my hand.

# The Last Seduction

*I had always thought Death beautiful. How
otherwise would she get the better of us?*

MARCEL PROUST

Everywhere, I'm reminded of her...
A fibrillating street-lamp, the winged demons
Of headlight glare,
The moon like an entry wound in the sky.

Her perfume crowds my nostrils.
Warm fragments of her image cling to the mirrors.
Her lips are so red, they seem always bleeding.
Her eyes enjoy the bewitching blue of light under snow.

And when she speaks, it is with the long slow sound
That waves make in darkness,
With the occasional flat note;
A blue interpolated minor third.

From a certain angle, the soft folds
Of her body resemble a secret landscape.
Solemn rises and skittish declivities.
Dark nameless places. A recession of beyonds.

Her clothes? Viscous silks. Touchable lustres.
Her walk? A callipygean swank.
With each self-forgetful stride,
She burnishes the world still further.

She cries as only a woman who believes in sin can cry.
Every street leads to her home.
The gravity of her warm mass drags me towards her –
To that nothing from which the universe is sprung.

And, tonight, the moon one night short of full,
I stand out in the open and feel
The wind flow like time around me,
Space warp as from the tug of a dark star.

# Metropolis

From the grubby purgatory of the U-Bahn
to the bulldozed rubble of Potsdamer Platz –
a titanic alphabet of cranes
and yellow earth-moving equipment.

The Soviets, Americans and British have given way
to MERCEDES, SONY and the department store HERTIE:
a corporate narcissism of self-regarding
office blocks at the city's heart.
If the city's soul were to generate mass
in the same way, it would sink,
superdense with its burden of history and guilt,
straight through to the other side of the earth.

Everywhere, the barriers are coming down.
In the hotel lobby, two lovers, nostalgic
for the Wall, enact their noon-time fetish,
speaking to each other from adjacent public phones.

Later, I see them together at the bar;
his hands composed around the stem of a glass,
the cunnilingual skin of a drink on his lip,
she running an index-finger down the length of his tie.

Alone, high in this room, giddy with inconsequence,
I watch objects assume different shapes in the dark,
and think of the little twist of the camera lens
necessary to make a wire fence disappear.

Over the EUROPA CENTRE, the MERCEDES-BENZ star
rotates like a weather vane.
Below, the red of tail-lights and the white
of oncoming beams: the drowned and the saved.

# Finishing Touches

He colour co-ordinates my clothes and cosmetics,
shampoos and combs my hair,
attends worshipfully to my fingertips,
depresses my shoulder carefully

and turns my body a little to the right.
He sponges me with talc
until my skin is oyster-white.
He is kind. I think he loves me.

He wires my jaw in place,
softens the curve of my shoulder,
gently cups my hands together
then bends towards my face.

My cheeks bloom florally
under the dabs of his brush,
my lashes delicate as the fuzz on a rose.
Consolingly, he strokes

the trembly shapes of my eyes
beneath closed lids,
parting my lips
ever so slightly

for a more life-like appearance.
For a moment his kisses burn.
One final time, I see him turn.
Then he goes home to his wife.

# Kaleidoscope

For hours, I sat
listening to my parents bicker
as a large vacuum-cleaner
scythed in broad sweeps
across the hotel foyer,
watching sharp patterns
resolve from fragments
of scattered glass
like clusters of stars
from light and dust –
observing flowers form
and brief symmetries
establish themselves
before another slow
twist of the instrument
saw the images dissolve,
the vacuum-cleaner
sashaying in giant arcs
across the foyer,
the revolving door of
the hotel spinning clockwise
on its axis, the little brushes
at the top and bottom
shirring against the floor
and ceiling, keeping
the cold air
out.